How To Write An eBook In 40 Days (Or Less)

By Brandy Miller

TokaySEO's books are available at special quantity discounts to use as premiums and sales promotions, or for use in corporate training programs. To place a bulk order, please contact the TokaySEO at info@tokayseo.com.

ISBN-13: 978-1483975467

ISBN-10: 1483975460
Printed in the United States of America

Table Of Contents

Dedication

Dedicated to my mother, Cheryl, my older sister, Darlene, to my husband, Randy, and my son, Eddie, and all those I have heard say, "I wish I could write a book." Now you can!

Preface

My name is Brandy M. Miller, and I am a professional Creativity Consultant for Creative Technology Services, the company I started with my husband last year. We work on graphic design, marketing, web design & development, custom applications programming, and – you guessed it – ghost writing, editing, and copywriting. I dreamed my whole life of becoming a writer. I have closets full of books on how to write, and I studied a lot of different techniques in articles and on blogs. None of that made me a writer. I became a writer when I made a commitment to myself that I was going to write.

Now, I get paid to write, and I write every day. I write on weekends and holidays and I enjoy doing it. I write both fiction and non-fiction. I write poems and songs. You can view some of my recent work at http://brandy-miller.blogspot.com.

I have participated in Nanowrimo for several years, and have now won it three times by completing a 50,000 word manuscript in 30 days. Two of these manuscripts sat in the bottom of my file drawer for years because I couldn't figure out a method for rewriting them to my satisfaction. Now that I know what needs to be done, I am in the process of rewriting them. I hope to have them up for sale in the next two months.

In the past 60 days, I have completed a book called Catholic Parenting: What the Catholic Church Teaches Us about Parenting. Midway through writing the book on Catholic Parenting, I jumped head first into Nanowrimo and began working on a 50,000 word book called The Chosen. I did all of this while ghost writing for a company and doing all of my other graphic design work. I am not telling you this to brag. I am telling you this so that you'll know I understand the challenges involved in writing.

Writing has meant making sacrifices in some areas of my life. I used to be an avid video game player, and I almost blew some of my college classes because I spent so much time playing them. My favorite game was The Sims, because I could be anything I wanted and do anything I wanted – including those things I thought were out of my reach in real life.

What I learned is that once I pulled myself out of the virtual world, I could get all of those things that I really wanted in my life by investing my time and my energy in what mattered most. I decided to stop living a virtual life and got a real life, and that's something you're going to have to do, too. You're going to have to make the commitment to put aside the TV programs you like to watch, close out of Facebook, and ignore the call of the video games. You're going to have to make a commitment to your future and write.

You can buy this book and then sit on it. I did that a lot in my younger years. I wanted it, but I didn't believe enough in myself to actually do anything about it. I bought the books and they sat on my shelves, thumbed through but not really read. You can do this. You do have the skill and the talent to accomplish this. You can write, and you can become a writer.

I promise you if you do everything that I instruct you to do in this book, you will have written a complete manuscript at the end of the day. I do not promise you that it will be ready for print. In fact, I will honestly tell you that it will need work before it's ready for publication. It will need editing and proofreading, at the very least. However, you will have a completed manuscript and the power that comes from knowing that you can do it. Once you've written one book and you've figured out what it takes, there's nothing to stop you from writing more books.

There Are No Short Cuts

If you thought this book was going to be a short cut to writing, you should ask for a refund right now. There are no short cuts to writing. I can outline for you steps you can take to help you get motivated and stay motivated. I can teach you techniques for pushing past writer's block and finding the endurance you need to go on, but I can't give you any shortcuts because there aren't any. Nobody, and I do mean nobody, can write this book for you.

You may find that odd to hear from a woman who ghost writes for a living. It's true, you can hire someone else to write, but then it's not really your book. You may own the rights to it, but you'll always know that you didn't write it. You will never gain the satisfaction that comes from true accomplishment. What you've basically done is become the kid who turned in someone else's homework. You won't know the content even if you get the credit for the grade, and come test time – the time when you need to apply that knowledge or use that skill or talk about that subject – you won't be able to do it. The bottom line is that you can't be a true writer until you pick up pen and paper or put the fingers to the keyboard and start writing.

If you're going to be a successful writer, I want you to accept the truth of this statement right now. You are going to have to make lots of sacrifices, give up lots of your free time, and commit yourself to writing. There is no other way around it, and no way to make it take less time except to write more.

That you're writing a book in 40 days is and should be seen as a major accomplishment. Most published authors take years to develop their manuscript. This is as short a shortcut as you can get, but it's still going to take you time, effort, and the willingness to sacrifice to get it all done.

Writing isn't a get-rich-quick scheme, so if you thought this book was going to tell you that you could write and become rich off your writing at the end of 40 days, get your money back. Writing the book in 40 days is just stage one of a much larger plan. There are still more steps involved. You'll need to rewrite the book, get it edited, publish it, and promote it. Once you've done all of that, there are plenty of ways to make money off a successful book with minimal extra effort, and that's one of the reasons people are willing to make the effort to write a book, but these things all take time. Don't expect to become the next J.K. Rowling with 40 days' worth of effort.

Whether you're writing fiction or non-fiction there are also no shortcuts when it comes to research. I wish there were. If you don't know a topic, haven't used an object, or haven't studied a subject you're going to destroy your credibility unless you take the time to do the research first. This is why, when writing a book in 40 days, I am going to instruct you to only pick a topic that you know inside and out – something that you can do or have done regularly. This is true whether you choose to do a fiction book or a non-fiction book. Besides, when you have the knowledge you're going to write with authority and you won't have trouble describing the item or process to your reader. You can write about something you don't know, but you need to be prepared to block out some additional time to do the research on that topic first, and this will slow you down.

Pray Over It

I started to leave this chapter out, after all I don't want to scare off people who aren't practicing believers, but the more I thought about it the more I decided that I was doing a real disservice to anyone who was trying to finish a manuscript in 40 days by leaving it out. Every time that I have been successful in completing a manuscript in a very short time frame (my latest book I wrote in 25 days!), I have started out by praying over it and kept praying over it throughout my work. I use a prayer developed by St. Thomas, however you can choose whichever prayer you like. You can even make a prayer up, after all the real purpose of prayer is to enter into a conversation with God.

One year, 10 days into my efforts to write a manuscript in 30 days, my hard drive crashed and I lost everything I'd done. With only 20 days left to finish, I had to make a decision on whether or not I was going to quit or push through. I decided to push through and start the book over. It was daunting, because I would need to write 5,000 words per day and I'd never done that much writing per day in my whole life. I knew that I would need to get some help if I was going to be successful.

For the next 20 days, I prayed every single day over that manuscript. Five days later, we did recover the hard drive and I was able to get my original work back. The amazing thing, though, was that my new stuff was even stronger than the old work had been. I was able to merge the two together to create a third story that was stronger yet. And, yes, I did finish everything on time.

If you're atheist or agnostic, you can ignore this step, but I encourage you to give it a try. There is ample scientific research to show that prayer – even prayer by an atheist or an agnostic – actually changes the brain. During periods of prayer, the back portions of the brain are quieted and the frontal cortex of the brain is stimulated. Prayer can bring peace, calm, focus, and an increase in creativity. These are definitely benefits that you will want to tap into and it doesn't cost you a thing to do it. If you decide to give this a try, I promise not to tell any of your atheist friends. Your secret will be safe with me.

It makes sense, too. Since God is the Creator of an entire universe, including over 7 billion human beings (counting only the living), not to mention all the animals, plants, insects, bacteria, and all the other things we find in our world there is no one who has more creative power than He does. Prayer allows you to tap into a portion of that creative power and make it your own. Plus, it meets the beginning writer's budget and time requirements: it's easy and it's free.

I make no secret of the fact that I'm Catholic. I left the faith at one point because I didn't know it, and I came back only because I found that all the answers to the questions I had were right there in the Catholic Church. I feel truly blessed to be Catholic, and one of the biggest blessings we have is Eucharistic Adoration. It's like sitting at the feet of Jesus. I can't point you to any studies on this, but I know that when I sit in front of the True Presence, I get some of my best inspirations and insights. Even if you aren't Catholic, I encourage you to look up the nearest Catholic Church offering Eucharistic Adoration and take the time to go. It can do a world of good for your writing. If nothing else, the calm, the peace, and the quiet will help you think.

Gather A Group

When you set out to write a book in 40 days is to gather together a group of supporters. Having a group of people who can support you in your writing is crucial to you finishing this book in 40 days. The ideal group would be other writers who are just as committed to helping you succeed as you are to helping them succeed, but any group will do. The only absolute requirement for this group is that they be positive and good cheerleaders, because you are going to need the encouragement.

If you think you can't possibly gather a group together, you probably already have a group. You probably already have a Facebook account or a Twitter account or some similar social media account. This can be your group. If you have a blog with some fairly regular readers, this is your group. The group does not need to be large. In fact, sometimes a small, tight-knit group is better than a large group. The point is that finding a group isn't hard these days. Social media makes it incredibly easy to find and become a part of a group.

If you don't have regular access to the internet, your group will need to be closer to home. Try your friends or your family, but remember that the people you select in your group need to be people who will believe in you. You will already have enough demons in your head telling you to quit and to give up, telling you that it's not worth it, doubting your ability to do it, doubting that you have anything worthwhile to say that anyone would want to read. The last thing you need is to have a real live person who says the same kind of garbage, because that's exactly what that is – garbage.

It's unfortunate but true that many of the people in our lives who are closest to us are the guiltiest of being the most negative and believing in us the least. Don't listen. You have a dream of being a writer or you won't be reading this book right now. You are capable of achieving this dream. You have a story inside of you that is worth hearing and worth taking the time to put on paper. You have skills and talents that you have a duty and an obligation to share. Your life is meaningful and your life has purpose. You are a worthwhile human being. Don't let anyone – and I do mean ANYONE – tell you otherwise.

If you can't find a single person in your life who is willing to cheerlead for you, I will. You can find me on Facebook or email me personally. I will read your work, cheer you on, and encourage you to finish. Why? Because you matter to me. I don't have to know you to know how important you are to the world. I know that if I get to know you, you're going to prove to be a wonderful person worth getting to know and worth being around. I also know what it's like to have to fight through other people telling you fifty million reasons why you can't do something, and you being the only one in the room who thinks you can.

Those people may care about you, but they are caught up in fear. Fear is false evidence appearing real, and it is the number one reason why people fail to achieve anything lasting. Their fear tells them that they can't succeed, so they don't.

You can succeed, and you will. You don't have to be held down by their fears.

I don't care if you've never succeeded at a single thing in your life before this moment. You can and you will succeed in writing a book in 40 days if you do everything that I ask you to do. You have everything it takes. All you have to do is tap into the good stuff inside of you to make it happen.

Make A Commitment

Make a commitment to your group. Make them a promise that you are going to be writing a chapter a day, every single day, for the next 40 days. You need to decide on, and commit to, an overall word length for your book and how long each chapter will be. I recommend targeting 1500 words per chapter, which gives you a finished book length of 60,000 words. Then make a commitment to hit that chapter word count mark every single day. If you think you can't hit 1500 words every day, but maybe you can do 500, commit to doing that. If you want to write your book in less time, obviously you'll need to increase your word count commitment.

I cannot stress to you how important it is that you make this commitment. I know you may have made commitments before, bigger ones than this, and you may have failed to live up to those commitments. You may not believe you can follow through on a commitment. However, all those failures were in the past. You are about to not just write a book, you are about to change your life. You are redefining yourself as we speak to become more like the person you want to be.

The person you want to be fulfills commitments, meets deadlines, sets goals, and achieves great things. The person you want to be is someone that others listen to and respect, and the first part of being respected is to live up to the commitments you make. People respect you when you show them respect, and you show people respect by fulfilling commitments you make to them. Fulfilling commitments shows other people that you value the relationship you have with them and that you are trustworthy.

Once you have made this commitment, I want you to think about everyone in your group anytime you are tempted to quit and give up. I want you to think about every single one of your readers that you have made this commitment to, and I want you to think about the kind of relationship you want to have with them. Do you want to be known as someone who keeps his or her word? Of course you do! This is where you begin to set the habits that will transform you into the kind of person others can rely upon.

The only reward this group of people who have assembled to cheer you on receives is your success. When you fail, you are telling them that their efforts on your behalf don't matter. Don't do that to them. They put the effort out to believe in you, to show up to your game, and to put on their pompoms and cheer you on. Honor that effort by pushing through and finishing when you feel like giving up.

If you have a bunch of people in your life who only cheer when you fail, or who won't cheer for you at all, don't let them stop you from succeeding – let them motivate you to prove them wrong. If you've failed to live up to your commitments in the past and people have stopped trusting and believing in you, let this be the opportunity you need to prove them wrong. You can make a commitment and you can see it through. You don't have to be held back by your past failures unless you want to be.

I am going to tell you something I have learned over the years, and it's something I want you to hold onto when you are getting discouraged or are tempted to beat up on yourself for the things you did wrong in the past. It does not matter how many times you failed. It only matters how many times you failed to get back up and try again. You have what it takes to succeed, but you have to take charge of your success and make it happen.

Maximize Your Time

It takes the average person 10 minutes to write 100 words, and so in order to be able to write the roughly 1500 words you will need to have your manuscript finished in 40 days, that means you need to find 150 minutes or about 2 hours of time each day to devote to your writing. This topic is actually a whole book by itself, I know because I just finished writing it, but if you are going to write a book in 40 days you will need to learn to all the help you can get to find the time you need to write it. Here is an overview of the advice you will find in my newest book, The Write Time: How to Find All the Time You Need to Write a Book:

Keep a Time Journal

Recording what you do and when is your first step in finding more time to write because it gives you a clear picture of what you are currently doing with your time, helping you to pinpoint areas that you can improve.

Block Your Time

You have 12 total 2 hour blocks of time in every day. 4 of those blocks, or 8 hours, should be spent sleeping, 2 should be given to eating & exercise, prayer and hygiene should take ½ block. This leaves you 5 ½ blocks for everything else you want to do. If you work 4 hours and commute 1 that means you're going to have to get creative with your time to find all of it that you need.

Combine Activities

Take a look at everything you do during a day and look for those things that you can combine together to free more time for your writing. For example, can you pray while exercising? Can you write during your lunch or breakfast time? Can you use your commute time to write by recording yourself talking your way through the material? Finding creative ways to combine the activities you do can free up extra writing time without compromising on the things that really matter.

Letting Go

It's quite likely that there are things you are doing every day that don't really need to be done. Eliminating these things during the 40 days you are writing will free up time. Common things you may be doing that are taking up time that could be spent writing are watching TV or movies, playing video games, or hanging out on social media. If you really want to get your writing done, you're going to have to let them go.

Make an Appointment

Every single day for the next 40 days, set an appointment with yourself for the time you are going to write. Treat it as you would any other appointment. Put it into your smart phone, mark it on your calendar, prepare ahead of time by packing the supplies you will need, and show up. It is okay to reschedule your appointment but don't cancel on yourself. Treat it as seriously as you would an appointment with a boss or client and allow absolutely no interruptions and no distractions during this time.

Develop Discipline

Daily decisions develop discipline. Make the decision each day that you will show up to your appointment. Every day that you do so makes it easier to show up the next day because you're developing mental muscles and habits.

Eliminate Distractions

Turn off or unplug the phone, disconnect from the internet, turn off the television, and go some place quiet. During your appointment time you want to make sure that you create an atmosphere that makes it as easy as possible for you to focus on writing. If you can, send the kids to the sitters or wait until they are in bed.

Avoid Time Sinks & Time Wasters

Plan your writing time in advance. Having an outline of what you are going to write about may seem stiff and rigid if you're writing fiction but it really can help you get more out of your time. Take 5 minutes to mentally envision the scene and then outline how things will go based on that visual. Don't check your email during your writing time and don't do research during your writing time. Both of these can seem like a good idea initially, but can also end up leading you down the rabbit hole and before you know it you'll have used up all your appointment time without having written anything.

Organize Your Work Space

Don't waste your writing time searching for something you need. Make sure everything you need is in easy reach.

Keep a bag for your writing appointments that keeps all of the information you need together including your outlines and your research.

Learn to Say "No"

You're going to have to politely say no to many things during this 40 days. Don't feel guilty for doing it, and don't make excuses. Explain that you'd love to say yes, but you wouldn't have the time you'd need to give this new project the attention it deserves.

These are just a few things that will help you find the time you need to write your book, but this will get you started.

Reward Yourself

Your brain is wired to be motivated by two things: pleasure and pain. Pain causes your brain to reject things, while pleasure causes your brain to desire more of a thing. If you're going to be successful in getting this book written, you are going to have to create your own personal rewards system.

One of the main reasons I tell you that you need to gather a group is that this group provides you with some important rewards in the affirmations they give you. Every time that you post a success and have other people respond positively, that tells your brain to keep going. It gives you the incentive you need to keep making the sacrifices you are making and to keep taking steps toward your goal. It's also the reason that it's so important that you surround yourself with positive people, people who are good at cheerleading and who genuinely believe in you. You need to know that all this hard work is going to pay off, and the affirmation of other human beings is proof of just that.

To complete my book on Catholic Parenting, I had to put down the remote and sacrifice watching some of my favorite TV shows. Therefore, I made my reward some TV watching at the end of each week. I knew that if I had accomplished my goals for the week, I would be able to watch my programs without feeling guilty. If I didn't, I would have to put off watching them until I had finished catching up. Given that I had all these other things to do, too, that might mean that I didn't get to watch my TV programs at all that week.

You really should have two types of rewards: rewards for minor goals and rewards for major goals. A minor goal would be finishing a chapter on time. A major goal would be finishing the first 10 days. You should also set a reward for accomplishing all 40 days of writing. This reward may be taking yourself out to dinner or spending a whole day playing your favorite video game, but it should be something very special and something you wouldn't ordinarily do.

When you get tempted to give up on your writing, or procrastinate on it, remind yourself of the reward that is waiting for you if you finish. If the reward is something like buying yourself a special treat, find a picture of that treat and hang it close to where you write. Look at the picture when you're tempted to quit.

I have finished several books, and I can tell you that I couldn't have done it if I hadn't set up some kind of system for affirming myself and encouraging myself to keep going. It's too easy to quit. There's so many things going on in your life that the excuses and the reasons why you can't will pile up. Giving yourself a rewards system is one more way you can ensure that you will see it through and succeed.

Our society isn't trained to deal with delayed gratification. We want things now, and usually we find ways to get them right away. We settle for fast food instead of the good stuff because we don't want to wait. We take on debt we later can't afford to pay because we don't want to wait to earn all the money for something. Writing, though, is a long term goal with a serious delayed gratification factor and there is no way around that. If you haven't been writing much before you decided to start this, you have to realize that you are doing the same thing as running a marathon with no training. If you're going to finish it in the 40 days, you're going to have to give yourself every tool you can to get it done.

Start With What You Know

No matter who you are, you have some life experience and now is the time to put that to use. This piece of advice is crucial if you are going to write this book in 40 days, because you aren't going to have the time to stop and research constantly. You're going to have to pull from what you've already done.

If you're writing a non-fiction book this means stopping and taking the time to assess what it is you do know. I don't want to hear you tell me you've never done anything and you don't know anything. Those are excuses. If you are old enough to read this book, you are old enough to have done some things. You have accumulated some knowledge. If you can draw, paint, sew, sing, or play a musical instrument, you have a skill that other people want to gain. Even if you don't think that you are very good at it, your skill level is higher than 0, which is where your beginner student is at. If you don't feel qualified to teach people, your experience puts you in a position to make referrals. Let people know how they can get started just like you did, what products or books or resources you would recommend.

If you collect something, this could be your topic. Explain how to get started collecting that item, or how to tell the value of the item, or what resources you use and you have found the contents of your potential book. If you are a student who gets good grades regularly, share your advice with other students on what to do so that they can improve their grades.

The bottom line is that you do have some information to share that someone will want to know. You may have to dig deep to find it, but it is there.

If you're having a hard time coming up with ideas for things to write about that would work with the life experiences you have to draw from, I recommend using Google's keywords tool. Type in a simple subject and see what Google returns as searches that other people have done using that subject. It might very well spark an idea for a book topic. It was in the middle of using Google's keywords tool to search for something else that I came up with the idea of writing this eBook.

If you're writing fiction, the process is a little different, but the advice is still the same. Write from what you know. Use places you've been to create the scenes in your book. Draw from the well of all the people you've met – whether you liked them or didn't – to flesh out the characters in your book. You can even create new characters based on the traits of two or three different people in your life to make a new one. This is your world, so it's up to you how you populate it.

If you've been in the work force for any time, even if it's just as a waitress or a cashier for a movie theater, you have an insider's view on how things operate. Include that insider's view in your writing. If you belong to a religion, you know what it's like to go to services and you can include descriptions of that in your writing. It may not be interesting to you, but it will lend authenticity to your character.

Everything you've done in your life is one more experience you can add to your book. Every place you've visited, every person you've met. You have a world of experiences that you can use to populate a book. You don't have to invent new ones to get great fiction. You just have to put the pieces of your life together from a different angle and with a new perspective.

(Non-Fiction) Create An Outline

Your next step after you've chosen a main topic is to create an outline for what you're going to write about each day. This is part of your commitment to your readers: that you will produce a chapter a day that will cover each of these areas. If you're writing it in a shorter time frame, you can either do two chapters a day or you can create less chapters but make them longer. It's up to you. You may think you can't possibly come up with 40 topic areas to cover, but I assure you it is possible and you can do it.

The trick is to spend time brainstorming. You're going to sit down at your computer, or with a note book and a pen, and you're going to list out every idea you can think of that's related to your main topic area. For example, if you are someone who likes to sew you can talk about picking a pattern, choosing fabric, types of fabric, designing fabric (if that's something you know about), choosing the right thread, laying out patterns, taking measurements, until you've collected double the number of topics as you have chapters.

Why double? You aren't going to use them all, at least at first. Save them, because you may use them later either to help you overcome writer's block or during your rewriting sessions. Some of them simply won't work, and you're going to need to trim the fat, so to speak. Either you don't have enough knowledge to speak about that topic or it doesn't really fit with your main idea, but not everything you come up with is going to work. The other reason to set out 80 topics is that it forces your brain to work hard to come up with ideas, and some of your best ideas are buried at the bottom. This will bring them to the surface.

Don't force the process. If talking about one thing sparks thoughts about another, related, concept write that down, too. You aren't saying no to anything yet, you're just allowing your ideas to come to the surface. If you get stalled out on ideas, go back to your Google keywords tool and type in some of the ideas that you've had. See what pops up under that idea as items that people have searched for information. You'd be surprised how quickly this will fuel more ideas.

Once you have your topics, go through the list and pick out your best ideas. If you find you like all of the ideas, see if there are ideas that you can combine together to form a stronger chapter and put these topics together. Usually, though, you will find at least some topics that just don't fit with the rest of them. Eliminate these, and use them at another time.

The next step is to organize those ideas. For example, if your topic is sewing you want to might want to talk about how to choose fabrics, pick a pattern, and purchase the notions before you start talking about cutting and laying out a pattern. If your topic is bird watching, you obviously want to talk about the supplies needed to be a good bird watcher before you have them jump into it. You probably want to finish your book with the advice about what to do should something go wrong. You might even organize it according to the most frequently searched topics, if you've been relying on Google keywords to come up with ideas.

Deciding on the order of the book is important because of how the brain handles storing of memories and learning. It does this by associating ideas together. The more closely related the ideas are, the easier it is for the brain to store and code that memory for easy recall or apply that concept. The more unrelated the ideas, the harder it is for the brain to make sense of the concept and the more likely it is that your reader will find it difficult to remember and apply. Since your non-fiction book is designed to teach people something or help them, it's important that it be ordered in a way that helps them to get the most out of your content.

(Fiction) Create A Backstory

Although there are a lot of books that tell you to pick your genre first, I respectfully disagree. Don't worry about deciding on a genre. Decide on a main character. Your task before you even start writing the main story is to focus on creating a life for that character. The reason I like to begin by generating a backstory for a character is that not only will it be helpful when deciding the genre – there are some characters who lend themselves better to fantasy novels than romance novels, for example – but it will help you to keep your story consistent. You will know not only how your character is likely to behave in any given situation, but why.

Another reason for beginning with your character's backstory is that it forces you to make some decisions about who your character is. You'll have already decided how old they are, where they live, when they live (nothing says you have to keep the story in the present day), whether they are married and have kids. Basically, in writing this short story about your character you will have already answered many of the questions about their life for yourself that the genre will really suggest itself.

A third reason to take the time writing the backstory is that it gives you room to pull up characters and events from their past if you get stuck while writing the story. I heard one piece of excellent writing advice from someone one time, advice that I have used to overcome my own writer's block. If you are writing a story and you get stuck – introduce a crisis or a new character. Either one will force your character to do some interactions and will move the story forward. Writing that backstory will give your character at least 5 people from their past that you can call upon anytime you get stuck.

There's no one way to write a character backstory. You can do it interview style, "day in the life" style, or just have the character describe themselves to you. When writing your character backstory, there are six basic questions you'll want to answer, no matter which method you choose to use to do it.

What's Their Problem?

The first thing you need to examine is what the problem is that your main character is facing. Every story's plot is driven by problems and the content of the story is how they try to resolve those problems, along with the obstacles they face and the setbacks they encounter along the way. It's the problems your main character faces and the ultimate resolution to that problem that determines the genre. For example, if Jack Stapleton's problem is that he must stop aliens from taking over his home planet, you have a science fiction novel. If Jack's problem is that he must stop pirates from boarding his vessel, you have a historical fiction novel. If Jack's problem is that he must stop dragons from destroying his village, you have a fantasy novel. You get the idea.

Who Are They?

Decide on their name, their gender, their age, their time and place of birth, and their appearance. What makes them unique? How do they see themselves? Is it the same as how others see them? Why or why not? These are the questions you want to answer in the process of creating your character's backstory so that you can fully describe them to your audience. Another part of deciding who they are is to explore their daily routine. What do they do every day? Where do they go and what do they see?

What Motivates Them?

After you decide who your character is, dive in to what they believe, what their fears and dreams are. Knowing what they believe can often inspire you to put them in situations that challenge their beliefs, or to include characters who ask them questions about their beliefs that give them and your reader an opportunity to explore what that means for them. It makes it easier to create heroic scenes and build empathy, too, as you force your character to face up to a fear in order to save the life of someone else or put aside their dreams in order to make someone else's dream a reality.

What Can They Do?

Taking the time to explore their talents, skills, knowledge, and experiences can suggest predicaments to put them in or even help you spot when your group of characters may need a little outside help. For example, maybe our hero Jack Stapleton has plenty of street skills but he's out in the wilderness trying to survive and everybody who is with him comes from the city. He's in a serious predicament and this can give you the excuse you need to introduce the heroine, who just happens to have grown up hiking in the woods and knows all about herbal lore, hunting, and tracking. The two may not get along at first because they don't understand one another, but Jack's dependence on her for food and shelter keeps him from leaving and her faith in God prevents her from abandoning him long enough that the two of them manage to fall in love.

Who Do They Know?

Who are the people in your character's life? You want to know as many of the past and present relationships as possible before you begin writing so that you can call upon these relationships at any time. Who are their friends? Who are their enemies? Who are their lovers? Any one of the people from their past can be called upon when you get writer's block as a tool to help you move the plot forward or change direction if you don't like where it's headed.

Who Are Their Relatives?

Our family relationships shape and form us. Those early relationships play out over and over again in our new relationships, and can go a long way to giving readers a good idea of why your character is the way that they are without you having to do the hard work of spelling it out for them. Plus, these relationships - both the ones they may know about and the ones they may be unaware of - mean you have a ready supply of people to bring out in the event of writer's block.

I recommend that you write at least 5 pages but not more than 10 pages for the character backstory. You don't want to get so caught up in writing the backstory that you never get started writing the real story, but you also want to have enough details that you can plug in those details whenever you need them. If you want help getting started with writing the character backstory, I have some character sheets which you can download for free at http://40daywriter.com/tools/character-sheets . You can also purchase my book, Creating a Character Backstory, first in my Fiction Writing for Beginners series, for more explanation of the topics I outline in this chapter and to help you get more out of the character sheets.

Write Every Day

In chapter 4, I told you that writing a book in 40 days is a whole lot like running a marathon. Just like any marathon runner, you need to get your muscles in shape and just as importantly you need to keep them in shape. Writing every day is what keeps your motivation up and your writing muscles worked out. It helps you to build the momentum that will take you to the finish line and give you the triumphant feeling of having accomplished something real and tangible.

There is another benefit to writing every day – it starts to build a readership. If people know that you're going to be releasing a new chapter each day, they will start reading. When I was writing my book on Catholic Parenting, my blog was only getting about 5-10 readers a day. That's pretty weak. When I started writing consistently, that number doubled, tripled, and even quadrupled until I didn't plan things as well as I thought I had and I was unable to access the internet and make posts for three days. My readership dropped like a rock and it took me a while to build it back up. Writing every day keeps your readers eager to see what is coming next.

I understand that your time to write may be the last hours of the day, when you're so tired you can hardly keep your eyes open. I've been there. Sometimes my writing time hasn't started until 10 pm at night, and I'm so tired that only God and spell check have kept me from making some pretty big bloopers, but I didn't let it stop me. You've made a commitment, and this is where you need to remind yourself that you are a person who fulfills your commitments. You don't want to let the people who believe in you and have invested in your success down.

If you do find that you aren't able to write one day, make it up the next day or as soon as possible. Do not quit. Do not give up, and do not abandon your goal. Writing is hard work. I'm not going to lie to you and say that it's easy, or everyone would do it. There are times when you may be frustrated, times when you may feel like you just don't have enough to say or that what you have to say isn't going to be heard above all the other people who are talking. This is not true.

There are hundreds and hundreds of artists in the world, but each one has something unique and special to offer because each and every one of them literally sees the world from a different point of view. No two human eyes see color the same way, because no two human eyes have the exact same number of cones and rods. You have a valuable message to share, and people will want to hear that message, but you first have to put that message into a format that will allow you to share it. So keep writing.

Don't worry if you think your writing stinks, or if it isn't the high quality you'd hoped it would be. What you are doing during this 40 day period is creating a more elaborate outline or fleshing out your character's story more. You will, as I told you earlier, need to go back and rewrite portions of the book you are writing. This is just the diamond in the rough.

Don't worry about polishing it, don't worry about cutting it yet. Just dig out the diamond by writing something each day.

When you made your commitment, you promised your readers that you would write a certain number of words each day. Make sure you hit that commitment before going to bed or doing anything else. There is nothing quite like going to bed feeling the satisfaction of having accomplished getting that chapter finished. You might secretly fear that you can't accomplish writing a book, but when you see that you can get that word count done each day, and then see that word count score raising higher and higher as you come closer to your goal, it's the proof you need to say, "Yes, I really can do this."

Moving Past Writer's Block

It happens to every writer. You lose motivation, you get tired, you don't feel like writing anymore, or you just can't think of enough words to fill the page. The difference between successful writers and people who only want to be writers is that successful writers don't let writer's block stop them from moving forward. They push past it and move on. You can, too.

If you're writing non-fiction, this is the time to turn back to your original list of topics. See if you can't add something to this chapter from that list. Obviously, you want it to make sense so it should be a related concept, but tie the two together to fill up the rest of your chapter. If that doesn't work, take a quick trip online and type in your chapter topic. See what comes up, read a few articles and see if something in those articles doesn't inspire you to write more. Another technique is to use the Google keywords tool just like you did when you were brainstorming to come up with ideas for things to talk about. Look up the things people most commonly ask on that topic and fill in the blanks with that.

Now, if you've done those things and you're still coming up short on your word count, open up a new window and just start writing whatever comes to mind on your subject. Start with the chapter's topic and brainstorm everything you can think of that is related to that topic. Don't edit anything yet. Take the topic and go over to Google's keywords tool and type in each idea, see what else pops up. Write those down. Once you've done that, pick out the 15 strongest items on your list and write 100 words about each topic. When you're finished, you'll have written all 1500 words. It's that simple.

If you're writing fiction, turn to your back story. What character from the past can you introduce into the current story? What place from the past can your character visit? Look through the backstory and look for details you've overlooked before. Have you failed to address a significant question about your character that's brought up by that detail? For example, maybe Marge Tatum only uses white teacups in her yellow kitchen. Does Marge have OCD? Does she feel that white is a lucky color for her? Are the white teacups something she inherited from a mother, a grandmother, or a favorite aunt?

For fiction writers, if you're still having trouble and the backstory hasn't provided you any new ideas, create a new character for your main character to interact with, a new crisis for them to resolve, or both. Do something that requires your character to react and respond immediately, to change directions, or reveals something new about them to you.

If you tried that and it still didn't work, take a clean sheet of paper or open a new window and just write down everything that comes to mind regarding the character, the setting, the plot, or the situation your character currently faces. Do not waste this time on negativity, or things like, "I think this story is dumb and I really don't feel like writing it anymore" unless you are prepared to ask yourself why you think it's dumb and what you are going to do to fix it. Your focus is to find some spark that gets things going again, some reason to fall in love with the writing all over again, because once you do you'll be past the writer's block and on to writing.

As you are brainstorming ideas, don't self-edit. Do not say that's a dumb idea or that would never work. It's your story and it can work if you want it to, so don't even concern yourself with that. Use the hot pen technique. Write freely for 10 minutes without allowing your pen to leave the paper and without stopping. Some of your best ideas can come out of this kind of writing.

Envision Success

If you are going to succeed in writing this book, you need to make that success a reality for yourself. You need to hold that vision of what it will look like to be successful in your head, especially when you are feeling the most discouraged and success seems least likely. If you are writing this book to prove to yourself that you can, imagine what it will feel like to be able to say to someone, "I wrote a book."

Imagine what the cover of your finished eBook will look like. What colors will you choose? What images would suit it best? One of the best things you can do is to spend some time collecting images of book covers that you think look good and would be a guide to how you want your finished book to look. Post those images near where you write and refer to them when you get discouraged or think about quitting. One of these days, a book cover will have YOUR name on it.

Imagine going to a class reunion and being able to tell those people who gave you the hardest time in high school, "I'm an author" when they ask what you do for a living. Most people spend an entire lifetime thinking about becoming an author, but you will have done it in only 40 days. You may not yet be a published author, but that's not the point. You've taken a huge step forward to achieving a dream that most people live a whole lifetime without ever doing.

Create a vision board to keep near your computer. If you don't want to do that, or don't have the space for it, use

Pinterest. On that board, you're going to pin images of what success will mean for you. Maybe it's a better car, or a bigger house, or maybe it's a first home. Maybe success will mean being quoted by someone else, or having your book appear on the New York Times Best Seller's List.

Your goal might be more modest. Maybe you are creating your book to help drive sales to an existing business, and your vision of success means more customers and more traffic to your website. Maybe you're creating that book to launch a speaking career. In those cases, imagine people calling your phone and asking for you to come speak to their organization, or telling you that they read your eBook and it really helped them.

Maybe success for you is just being able to give your child something to remember you by. Maybe you're writing a book for him or her. Envision reading that book to your child each night, and seeing the sparkle in their eyes because they know that this book is a visible sign of your love for them. Maybe you are writing this book as an anniversary gift to your spouse. Imagine their amazement as they read the book that represents all the love you have for them. How will this add to your relationship?

Maybe you'll use this book as an elaborate means of proposing to the person you love most. Can you imagine the look of surprise and delight on your intended's face when they realize that the chapter headings spell out "Will You Marry Me?" or something similar. Imagine sharing this eBook as a wedding gift to those who attend your wedding, or even to the wedding party.

Whatever it is that your book is intended to do, create that vision in your mind and hold on to it. Do not let anyone or anything rob you of your vision. It is possible, you can do it, and there are rewards waiting for you when you succeed. All you have to do is hold on to the belief long enough, take steps every day to make it a reality, and it will happen.

Recovering From Failure

At some point in time, you are going to set out to write a book in 40 days or less. You're going to do everything I've instructed you to do. You're going to line up a group, make the commitment, write the outline or create the backstory, and then you're going to start writing with the best of intentions and a lot of high hopes. However, something's going to get in your way and you're going to miss your deadline. You're going to fail, and you're going to let everyone down. This chapter is written for just such an occasion.

The first step in recovering from failure is to acknowledge that you did fail. You made a mistake, took a tumble, and got sidetracked. It happens. You're human. Realize that it would be more shocking if you never failed than it is that you did fail. Relax, and take a deep breath. As long as you follow these next steps in recovering from you failure, there's still a bright future ahead of you.

The second step in recovering from failure is to admit that you failed without any varnish. Don't excuse your failure. You can explain it, but don't excuse it. Your friends and support team deserve to know what happened, and the longer you leave this step undone the greater the amount of guilt and shame that will build up. Guilt is not a bad thing in and of itself. It reminds us that we need to do some relationship mending, to take some action to fix what we've broken. However, allowing guilt to fester causes it to turn into shame. Shame tells you to hide your failures and not admit to them.

Shame keeps you from moving forward. Shame is the enemy of every author and every person who ever tried to do anything great. Admitting that you failed to your friends and support team prevents shame from creeping in and stealing your dream. It gives you a chance to receive the forgiveness and encouragement you need to get back up again and move on.

The third step in recovering from failure is to figure out what went wrong. What caused the problem? Were you distracted by a holiday? Did life take an unexpected turn of events? Did you fail to manage your time properly? Did you just lose your motivation or your inspiration? Until you pinpoint the source of your failure, you won't be able to make a plan to avoid a repeat of that failure. Once you have figured out why you failed in your initial attempt, devise a plan that takes that problem into account. If you found that the problem came from your writing taking longer than expected to finish, rebudget your time accordingly. If you found that you lacked motivation, record a tape of positive affirmations and play it to yourself once a day every day. Whatever the problem, there is a solution.

The fourth step is to renew your commitment. You've made a mistake and you broke your initial commitment, but that doesn't mean you can't make a brand new commitment and start over again. Failures become temporary setbacks unless you allow them to become permanent by refusing to overcome them. So, renew your commitment to your friends and support team. Write out a contract to them and sign it. Then hang that contract right by your computer or writing space. Look at it every time you are tempted to quit or give up.

The fifth step is to get back to writing, and start today. There is nothing that will restore your confidence and shorten the recovery process like writing. The failure can cause you to doubt that you are capable of doing this, and only writing something will prove to you that you can. So pick up the pen, or put your fingers on the keyboard and get to it, already! Your audience awaits.

Take A Break

You've completed your book. You've got roughly 50,000 words written, and you are feeling GREAT! You're ready to conquer the world, and nothing seems impossible. You're wondering what to do next. Here is my advice: Take a break. Put your manuscript away for at least 30 days. Do nothing with it. Don't even think about it. Just leave it be.

When I studied art in college, one of the first things I learned about was the effective use of negative space. Negative space is the "quiet" part of the canvas, the area where there is no artistic activity happening. Without negative spaces on a canvas, everything just blends into one another and there is no definition between objects. Your brain works the same way. You need to create negative spaces in your life, times when it is quiet, relaxing, and nothing is going on, so that your brain can recharge and put together all of the experiences you've had to make new connections and generate new ideas.

If you are feeling anxious that taking a break will cause you to lose those writing muscles you've worked so hard to build, keep writing. Taking a break from your novel doesn't mean you have to take a break from writing in general. One suggestion on what to write during this time is to journal. Simply write about your life over the next 30 days, noting the experiences you have and the people that you meet. Write for fun, write simply to enjoy it, and just allow your brain to wander.

Another potential suggestion for what to write during this time is to write about your past. Pick a person, an object, or a location from your personal past and write about that. Write in fine details, recreating the scene in your mind and exploring how you felt, what you saw, what you smelled, and what you tasted. What season was it? What time of day? Be as detailed as possible. These exercises can help you, not only when it comes time to rewriting your novel, but in future writing endeavors as well.

A third suggestion for something to do to keep the creative juices flowing without working on your novel is to go people watching. Visit a location where there are lots of people to observe, such as a mall or a park. Write down what you see them do, what they were wearing, and what makes them unique from the rest of the people around them. Use that basic description to come up with a short story around that person. These short character sketches can become fodder for characters in later writing and will start building up a library of people to help you populate the worlds you create in your stories.

A fourth suggestion is to read the news. Make a note of headlines that particularly interest you and write a short story around that headline. Don't read the actual story, create your own. What, exactly, happened? Where did this headline take place? When did it happen? Who was involved? How did the reporter find out? Is the reporter's story accurate and complete, or is there more to the story than the reporter knows?

A fifth suggestion for things to keep you writing while you're taking a break is to visit interesting places or go out and view interesting objects in your town. Write a story about those places or objects. If you wish, you can research the history of the object and incorporate that into your story, or you can create a whole new story about it based entirely on whatever your imagination can bring to mind.

You'll know when you've taken a long enough break from writing that particular novel when the details are no longer sharp and in focus anymore. This is the time to get back to work, because it means that you can now look at your work more objectively.

Tips For Rewriting

You've done it! You've written a book in 40 days. You have dared to do what few men or women are brave enough, dedicated enough, or just plain crazy enough to do. No longer will you sit in your arm chair thinking, "Someday, I'm going to write a book" because the truth is you've just done it! You can proudly proclaim to friends, family members, jerks from high school, and anyone else who will listen that you are an author. You may not be published yet, but that doesn't make the fact that you are an author any less true.

However, at some point in time you are going to want to stop patting yourself on the back long enough to get down to rewriting and shaping that book for publication. These are some tips for what to do next.

Non-fiction: What research can you include to support your claims? Who could you interview that might lend your book credibility? Who do you know that is an expert in that topic that would be willing to read and review the book for you? Are there tables, charts, or graphs that you could add to make it more attractive and enticing?

Fiction: Read your manuscript from cover to cover. Anytime there is something interesting about your main character or one of your supporting characters that is brought up but never mentioned again or dealt with, make a note of that. Write a story about your character and that particular incident. Reread your manuscript with that story in mind and see if you can't work it in to something interesting. If there are characters in your book that seem flat or that lack distinguishing characteristics, write a backstory for that character describing how they met your main character and what that first meeting was like. Then go back and rewrite the scenes with this new information.

Check for story integrity. Make sure that your character never does anything or says anything that isn't consistent with the backstory you wrote for them. Write a timeline of the events in your book, and be sure that every scene is placed correctly in time.

Look out for pet phrases. These are phrases you use over and over again throughout your writing without being aware of it. If you catch yourself using a phrase more than once, highlight the phrase and use the find and replace function in your word processing program to find every instance that you've used it. Then, rewrite those passages.

When you think you've gotten the book large enough, long enough, and interesting enough to be published – go back to your group. Ask each of them to proof read it, ask questions about it, and tell you their honest opinions. You don't need people to be nice to you, you need them to be honest because your audience certainly will be.

Editing Your Masterpiece

Editing isn't just about fixing grammar errors or spelling mistakes. It's actually about looking at your book objectively and figuring out where it could be improved. This is why you need to take quite a bit of time away from your manuscript so that you can look at it from a brand new perspective. It's easy to get attached to your book the way it was written, to fall in love with it and to be reluctant to make changes because you think it is both awesome and amazing. However, I will tell you now that every book you write will need editing of some sort or another because you can always make something better.

For Non-Fiction Writers

One of the most helpful techniques for non-fiction writers is to look for 5 to 6 themes that the chapters could fall into and see whether or not your current order reflects that theme. As an example, when I was writing The Write Time, I ended up choosing the themes of motivation, preparation, planning, implementing, staying on track, and overcoming obstacles. When I looked at the book chapters with those themes in mind, it immediately became clear to me that I needed to rearrange some of the chapters in order to create a more coherent picture for readers.

For Fiction Writers

The single best way to figure out whether your story makes logical sense is to deconstruct it. Break it down into an outline format. If you aren't sure how to do this, in my blog on http://40daywriter.com I show you how to do it using the story of Little Red Riding Hood. Your story is going to be a lot longer than Little Red Riding Hood, but the principles work the same. Break the book into 3-5 different "Acts" and tie a theme to those acts. Then break each act into 3-5 scenes, and each scene into 3-5 events. For each event, note which characters appear in this event. Does everything make sense? Does everything work well together? Is there anything in there that's unnecessary? If there is anything unnecessary, get rid of it. If there is anything that doesn't make sense where it currently sits, see if it would work better either altered or moved.

Get Help

You are not going to be able to spot every mistake on your own. You should either talk someone you know into helping you edit the story and provide you feedback on what they think could be improved, or else pay someone to read it for you. There's a site called fiverr.com which has plenty of people out there who are willing to do just about anything for $5, including edit a book for you. Review their work, look at their reviews, and then hire one or several people to read it and make suggestions. You don't have to take all of the advice that is offered to you, but make a note of it if more than one person makes a comment about a particular spot in your book because that's something you really do need to address right away.

Publishing: Traditional VS Self-Publishing

If you've gotten your book just the way you want it to be, and you think it's ready to be put out into the wide world for readers to explore, you have choices to make. You need to decide on whether you are going to self-publish or go the traditional route. There are advantages and disadvantages to both, and I'll go into a little bit of detail about that here.

Traditional Publishing

Traditional publishing leaves most of the power in the hands of the publishing company. They get to decide whether or not your manuscript ever sees the light of day. They get to suggest or insist upon edits and title changes and a thousand other details. You can spend years trying to find someone who is willing to publish your manuscript, and at least another year or two working with the publisher to prepare the manuscript for its first print run. You also do not get to keep all of your royalties. You may give up 70% or even 80% of the royalties for each book you sell to the publisher. This can be a tremendously daunting prospect for someone who just wants to get their manuscript out there, but there are advantages to the way things are done.

When you go with a traditional publishing house, you have less work to do in terms of the editing and proof-reading. You also have a team of experienced people who will help you come up with a cover design, who will help you to promote the book, and who will act on your behalf to get your book into bookstores. The difficulty involved in getting a manuscript picked up by a traditional publishing house is so well-known, that when you manage this feat you gain instant credibility in the eyes of those who read your work. People trust books published by traditional publishing houses more than they tend to trust independent authors and publishers because they know that traditional publishers pour thousands of dollars into getting a book just right before they release it for sale.

Self-Publishing

The joy of self-publishing is that you are firmly in the driver's seat. You don't have to wait for someone else or experience the pain of rejection letters. You can take your book from first draft to final draft in a matter of days if you really want. You get to keep everything. You don't have to split your royalties with the publisher. You alone get to reap the rewards of all your hard work.

On the downside, you are responsible for everything. You must make, or hire someone to make, a cover for you. You must either create your own layouts or hire someone to do it for you. You must not only edit your own work but you are also the one who will be promoting it. If you know nothing about marketing, you're going to have to learn and you're going to have to learn quickly. You will have to work twice as hard as the standard publishing house to earn the trust of readers and gain reviews. You will have to schedule your own book signings, working directly with book stores to get their attention. You will have to fight to get your books on the shelves of major retailers who are already crammed full of thousands of other books and who may not be friendly to independent publishers like yourself. All of this takes time, money, and work. This is time, money, and effort you are not going to be able to put into writing your next book.

Another Possibility

There are independent publishing houses out there, start-ups who are eager for authors to sign. Sure, you may not get a signing bonus and you are going to have to split your royalties with them, but it does reduce the amount of work you have to do in terms of layout, editing, proof-reading, and cover design. They will also help you to promote your work, although the honest truth of the matter is that you're still going to want to do a lot of your own promotional work because they may or may not have the resources to devote to doing it. Working with an independent publishing house is a whole lot like getting a partner in your writing business. The two of you are in it together, from start to finish. This is actually the route I ended up going with after having tried my hand at self-publishing. I still design my own covers, but that's because I'm a graphic designer by trade and it's good for my business.

Whichever Direction You Choose

No matter which way you go with your publishing, it's not going to be a matter of simply putting it into the right hands and walking away, expecting the checks to flow in each month on their own. You are going to absolutely have to commit yourself to promoting your book before the sales are going to start flowing. The big publishing houses do not exempt you from this need. Your publisher has only a limited budget to spend on your book's promotion, so if you want your book to continue generating revenue long after that budget runs out, you need to be out there promoting it as far and wide as you possibly can. Don't worry, though, we'll discuss some ways you can begin doing that in the next chapter.

Self-Publishers: Amazon VS Smashwords

There are a lot more options for publishing your finished eBook than this, but these are two of the heaviest hitters in the field. I'll discuss a few of the advantages and drawbacks to each, but ultimately it is up to you to decide which route to take.

Amazon

Amazon is probably the single most visited site for book purchases on the internet, with millions of visitors from countries all over the world coming to their website. This gives you a huge amount of potential traffic if you can tap into it, but that climb to the top isn't easy because this also means there is a ton of competition for that same traffic.

It costs you absolutely nothing to join the Kindle Direct Publishing revolution, which makes your book available not only on every Kindle device but also available in their desktop Kindle emulator. As long as you price your book between $2.99 and $9.99, you will get to keep 70% of the revenues made from book sales. Price it higher than that, and you get to keep only 30%. The main drawback - and it is a considerable one - is that you are required to offer your book exclusively on the Kindle for 90 days. This means you can't tap into other markets, can't offer it for sale on your own website, can't give it away except during your 5 free kindle days, and you can't have it up anywhere else that an internet connection might reach.

Now, having said that, a lot of publishers find it worth the sacrifice to gain access to Amazon's traffic sources. The 5 free kindle days are absolutely crucial, though, to gaining traction for your book. Schedule it 30 days into your 90 days to give yourself enough time to list the book on as many free ebook listing sites as possible. During those 5 free days, Tweet your book offering at least twice a day each day it's out for free. What you want during this time is for the reviews to begin coming in because it's the reviews that will really help keep those book sales going. Post your free book offerings as an event on Facebook and invite everyone you know to the "party". It really is that crucial. Encourage reviews, ask for shares and retweets, and push your book as many places as you can think of during those 5 free days.

There's a second reason, aside from the reviews, that you want these people to download that book. Every time that someone does download it, Amazon counts it as a purchase. Your book is now linked to every book they've ever read or downloaded to their Kindle. This means that anytime someone pulls up a book in their database, your book has a chance of appearing in that section entitled "People who bought this book also bought", Amazon's way of suggestive selling. That means your book ends up getting an even broader exposure than it might otherwise, and can help continue pushing sales long past the 5 free days.

The third reason is that if you can generate enough downloads of your book, you get to go on the list of best sellers under the free books category. This can provide you an incredible amount of additional exposure since a lot of people specifically search out these top lists, presuming that the high rankings mean higher quality books.

Smashwords

Smashwords is also free to list, and while it doesn't have the massive amount of traffic that Amazon does, that doesn't mean it doesn't have a significant amount. Furthermore, Smashwords provides you a free ISBN number, no restrictions on how or where you can list your book or what you can do with it, and automatically translates your book into one of the widest varieties of electronic publishing formats I have seen, from epub to mobi to pdf and beyond.

Once your book has met all their qualifications, they will add it to their extended distribution catalog - meaning that it can appear in the Apple Store, Barnes & Nobles, and Amazon. You keep 85% of the royalties, and they do have provide coupons that you can use to help promote your book. The nice thing about coupons is that they allow you to not only see how many people have cashed in on a free offer but which advertisement you have put up is drawing the most traffic. That kind of information is solid gold when it comes to book promotions.

The downside to using Smashwords is that its meatgrinder application (the software that transforms your word document into an ebook) does not handle images at all, and it is super picky when it comes to formatting. You also can't put affiliate links in your book because you never know where the content will end up and many retailers reject anything linking back to another bookseller for very good reason. It also does not have the traffic that Amazon can command. However, it can still be a good option to use it just means you'll have to work a little harder to promote your book.

Promoting Your Book

Promoting your book should begin while you're in the editing phase, before your book is ready. It starts with picking a good, strong title for the book. You want something that does not have a duplicate on Amazon already. You want something that is memorable and that promises only what you will deliver inside the pages of your book. The title of Dragon's Desire is all fine and good, but if somebody starts reading your book and finds that not only are there no dragons in it, but there's not even any desire in it, they are perfectly within their right to be unhappy and leave you a poor review no matter how well your book was written. A title that promises one thing and delivers another is like using an ice cream scooper to put mashed potatoes on top of an ice cream cone. People may love mashed potatoes, but they are going to say, "Gross!" when they taste it because it's not the taste they were expecting.

Register Your Domain

Once you have chosen your book's title, and this is true regardless of the publishing route you've chosen, register the domain name for that book. You then want to build a website to help promote and support your book. This website does not have to be complex. You need nothing more than a page devoted to describing the book and its contents, a page that tells them something about the author, a calendar, and a blog. That's it. Super simple, and very easy to set up and maintain. The blog keeps your website fresh in the eyes of Google and gives your potential readers a reason to come back. The calendar is where you will advertise your book signings, speaking engagements, appearances, events, and (for Amazon KDP publishers) your free book days.

Build a Following

Start building a Twitter following. There are sites that claim to be able to buy 10,000 fans or more for $25, but I can't recommend that strategy because I know nothing about how it works or about its reliability. My thoughts are that people who pay for Twitter followers aren't likely to be building the kind of loyal following you need to generate book sales. Here are the techniques I have used to begin gaining followers:

1) Search for topics relevant to your book

If you're writing a romance, you might see if there are conversations going on under #romance or #romancebooks.

2) Tag your posts

Use hash tags (#) in front of words to make them searchable by others. This can make you easier to find and lets people know the kinds of things they can expect from your Twitter feed.

3) Follow others

Follow as many people as you can. At least 25% of them will likely follow you back. Don't limit yourself to following just those who are in your industry. The more people you follow, the more chances a tweet of yours will get retweeted and the broader the audience you have the potential of reaching.

4) Participate in the conversations

Actively engaging with others is quite possibly the best way to gain new followers. My husband has personally been retweeted by celebrities because of his interaction with them.

5) For Facebook

Use giveaways - either autographed copies of your book or something similar - to attract the likes you want, and encourage your followers to post stories about their experience with the book. Encourage them to share by offering special prizes for those whose posts get the most likes and shares. These featured stories help build credibility in a way that no amount of talking about yourself can.

6) For Pinterest

Have readers snap pictures of themselves reading your book & post to their Pinterest wall. Have a special giveaway for those who have the most creative picture.

Get to Know Book Store Staff and Owners

Getting to know the staff and the owners of the book stores in your area can go a long way toward helping you arrange your book signings when the time comes. Be nice to ALL The store employees, not just the ones who draw the biggest paychecks. Cashiers spend more face time with customers than anyone else and are often asked their recommendation for which books to buy. Stockers are responsible for product placement and will remember the author who treated them well.

Reach out to writer's groups & book clubs

Reach out to writer's groups and book clubs, and then get involved. If you already belong to a writer's group, suggest that you reach out to nearby writer's groups to offer cross-promotion opportunities, create a speaker's exchange, and attend one another's events. For book clubs, find out what their guidelines are for new book submissions and follow them. If the book club is local, or is in an area where you are doing a book signing, offer to attend their club to allow them to do a question & answer session, either as a fund raiser for the group or as a perk of membership. These work for online and offline book clubs and writer's groups. Make sure that you are giving back to these groups at least as much as you are asking them to give.

BookBuzzr

I don't have any affiliation with this site, but they did a great job helping me to generate sales for my book, Creating a Character Backstory, and so I'm recommending them. I recommend the $24 a month package. It's probably one of the best investments you'll make in terms of promotional bang for the buck. If you have sell at least 12 copies a month through them you'll have made your money back in most cases, and I sold 5 copies just using the tools at the basic package without the additional promotional exposure offered at the higher levels.

Getting More Out of Your eBooks

The publication of an eBook isn't the end of your opportunities for making money and gaining authority, it's just the beginning. There are plenty of things you can do to get more out of your eBook without putting a whole lot more time, energy, and effort into getting it done. A lot of these directly apply to non-fiction writers, but can be creatively applied to fiction writers as well. Here are just a few of them.

Transform your eBook into webinars

I recommend doing one 30 minute webinar that starts with a 5 minute introduction and ends with a 10 minute question & answer session, then spends 15 minutes giving attendees a fly-over view of your book. You're not going to have a lot of time to dabble in specifics, which is perfect for generating additional interest in your content as well as building up a fan base for your ebook. Then, break down your book into 5 segments and do a webinar for each of those 5 segments. You can either monetize these or use them to target your marketing towards different audience segments who might be interested in your eBook's overall content.

If you are a fiction writer, you may be thinking that it would feel odd to host a webinar based on your material, so you might want to focus here instead on creating a "behind the scenes" style webinar. Not only will this webinar likely to be of great interest to your fans, but aspiring authors can learn a lot from seeing how you transform your ideas to make the magic that becomes a fiction book.

Turn webinars into seminars

Once you have the materials in place to do webinars, you are ready to host your first single day seminar. The ideal set up for your seminars is to have 8-10 attendees at round tables. After they listen to your 15 minute talk, you give them 20 minutes to discuss it as a group and then another 20 minutes to do a group activity that reinforces your content. Not only does this help your attendees get more out of the content and see new ways to apply the material, but it's fun and takes a whole lot of the pressure off of you to be engaging for an entire day.

Create video content

Create a video course out of your webinars and seminars by recording them and then giving those who watch your series at home a set of exercises they can do by themselves or with a group of friends. These videos are a great way to extend the reach of your content and grow your authority.

Record your ebooks

Take the time to make audio recordings of your ebooks. Commuters especially enjoy these as they provide a way to make the most of their free time. It also makes your content available to those who are visually impaired or who are auditory, rather than visual, learners.

Dive Deeper

For non-fiction book writers, create a new ebook for each chapter you wrote in your original eBook. Undoubtedly there was content you could have included that you left out for the sake of time or because it didn't really fit with the original content theme. This is the time to take that content out, dust it off, and put it back in to your new eBook.

For fiction writers, this is the time to explore in greater detail scenes you didn't have a chance to do more than brush past before now. You also have a chance to tell the story or explore the world from a different character's point of view. If you have an audience who loves the world you built, you have a group of readers who are hungry for this exact kind of material.

The author would like to offer her thanks to you for taking the time to read this book. If you have enjoyed the contents, please take a moment and leave a review on Amazon. This is one of the best thank you's that you can give any author, and it only takes a few seconds of your time.

You can find additional help with your writing by visiting her at http://40daywriter.com

You can also connect with her online through Twitter: @WriterBrandy

Like us on Facebook: https://www.facebook.com/pages/How-to-Write-an-Ebook-in-40-Days-or-less/160919860740327

www.ingramcontent.com/pod-product-compliance
Lightning Source LLC
Chambersburg PA
CBHW070605290526
45790CB00002B/793